Dealing with
GIANTS

GREG LAURIE

 Dana Point, California

Dealing with
GIANTS

Unless otherwise indicated, all Scripture quotations are taken from the New King James Version. Copyright © 1982 by Thomas Nelson, Inc. Used by permission. All rights reserved.

Scripture quotations marked (NLT) are taken from the *Holy Bible*, New Living Translation, copyright © 1986. Used by permission of Tyndale House Publishers, Inc., Wheaton, Illinois 60189. All rights reserved. Quotations marked (NIV) are taken from the Holy Bible, New International Version®. NIV®. Copyright © 1973, 1978, 1984 by International Bible Society. Used by permission of Zondervan Publishing House. All rights reserved. Scripture taken from the New American Standard Bible® (NASB), Copyright © 1960, 1962, 1963, 1968, 1971, 1972, 1973, 1975, 1977, 1995 by The Lockman Foundation. Used by permission. Scripture quotations taken from the Amplified® Bible (AMP), Copyright © 1954, 1958, 1962, 1964, 1965, 1987 by The Lockman Foundation. Used by permission.

ISBN 0-9762400-9-2

Printed in Canada.

Published by: Kerygma Publishing–Dana Point, California
Coordination: FM Management, Ltd.
Cover design: Christopher Laurie
Editor: Larry Libby
Copyediting: Nancy Taylor
Interior Design, Production: Highgate Cross+Cathey, Ltd.

Contents

1 ❘ GIANTS
in Your Life

Do you have any giants running loose in your life right now?

Chances are, you do.

Most of us have at least one or two—kicking down our fences and stomping brazenly across the middle of our landscape or lurking just over the horizon, waiting to make their move.

What do I mean by a "giant"? I'm talking about those seemingly insurmountable problems and issues life sometimes brings our way.

Perhaps it's a giant called *Fear*.

Maybe there's something out there, something dark and sinister prowling around the perimeter of your life in recent days that absolutely terrifies you. Every now and then you feel its long shadow fall across your day, and fear grips your heart. Or you sense it looming close in the middle of the night, somehow deepening your darkness, and robbing you of your sleep.

And even though it retreats a little sometimes, stepping into the background, it never goes completely away.

Or maybe it's a giant of *Personal Sin*. You have an area in your life that continually defeats you, keeps you in bondage, and steals your joy. No matter what you do, no matter how you've prayed, no matter what you've tried, you just can't seem to defeat this thing.

Sometimes you think you've pushed it away or forced it into submission. A few days go by. Maybe even a few weeks. Sometimes you will even get through a whole month and begin to breathe a sigh of relief. And just that quickly it comes roaring back with a vengeance, wrecking havoc just as though it had never been away. You hear its taunting laugh, a laugh that shakes the windows of your soul, and you wonder, *Am I ever going to be free from this?*

It might be a giant named *Addiction*—one of the ugliest, most evil giants you could ever face. You've been trying to break free from it for months. Even years. Or decades. And this intruder in your life has been mocking you and defeating you day after day. You've fought and you've battled, you've wept and you've pleaded, but it only seems to loom larger with the passing of time.

You may be addicted to illegal drugs or prescription painkillers. It may be alcohol. You've tried the treatment programs, you've practiced all the techniques, you've read the books and pamphlets, but the giant grips you with iron fingers, squeezing the very life out of you.

There are all kinds of giants skulking around out there, with names like Pride, Envy, Gossip, Greed, Gluttony, Lust, and Pornography. In some cases, it's as though they have taken up residence in your life—made themselves at home. And in your heart, you've almost come to the conclusion that you'll have to live with that gross giant the rest of your life.

Sometimes the giant is some heavy, pressing issue you're facing in your life—something you can't seem to find an answer for or get resolved. Maybe it's a spouse who doesn't know the Lord. And as the years go by they don't seem to be any closer to coming to faith. In fact, in some ways they seem further off than ever. Maybe it's a prodigal son or daughter. You've been praying for him or her to come back to the Lord, but there has been no response, no hopeful signs, no turning. In fact, it may even seem like they are getting worse. And you wonder, *How am I ever going to overcome this? Will this giant ever go away?*

So how do you deal with a giant, anyway?

It's a handy thing to know. It's good information to stick in your back pocket in case you encounter one along your path or feel one shaking your house in the middle of the night. We're going to look at some answers together in the next few pages, drawing them from the life of David.

A big, ugly Philistine named Goliath was certainly one of the giants that crossed David's path, but he wasn't the only one. By learning how God enabled this young man to cut giants down to size, we will gain the faith and confidence to face those towering adversaries of our own.

2 | *Prepare Your Heart for* **BATTLE**

The choice of David to lead Israel was a shocker. No one saw it coming. No one, and I mean no one, would have had him on their long list, let alone their short list, for the next king following Saul.

Just before Saul took the throne, the Israelites had begun clamoring for a king to lead them in battle, just like all the other nations around them. Prior to that, the Lord had ruled His people through godly judges He raised up according to His choosing—heroes like Gideon, Deborah, Samson, Ehud, Samuel, and others.

The prophet Samuel was Israel's last judge, and a mighty man of God. But as he grew old, his countrymen took note that Samuel's sons had disqualified themselves from leadership by their sin and reprobate lives. Without a natural choice for the next judge before them, the people started looking around, and they came to the conclusion that they wanted a king "because everyone else had one." (Bad reason.) The Philistines had kings. The Edomites had a king. The Moabites had a king. The Amonites had a king. The Egyptians had a king. It was the global expectation that every nation would be led by a king, and they wanted one too.

They wanted a big, strong, handsome king who would really look the part and give them a good feeling when he was out front leading them in battle. And because they insisted, God said yes. He gave them exactly what they asked for.

And that's not always a good thing.

You remember the old saying? Be careful of what you wish for because . . . you might get it! Well the Israelites got it. God gave them a king who was suited to their desires and fulfilled their image of what a king should be. You might say that he was a man after man's own heart. His name was Saul.

The Bible tells us that initially, Saul had a lot going for him. He was from a good family. He was tall, strikingly handsome, and in the beginning, blessed with a humble spirit. We even read that God's Spirit came upon him for the task at hand.

It looked so good . . . for a little while. (Actually not very long at all.) Almost right off the bat King Saul began to self destruct. It started sort of small, then began to snowball. And before Saul had really become established on the throne of Israel, God had already rejected him from being king. Not only that, the Lord had gone ahead and selected a new man to take his place.

It was as though the Lord was saying, "All right, you wanted a king after your own heart, and I gave him to you. And you can see what you've got. Now it's My turn. I'm going to make the choice. I'm going to choose a man after *My* own heart."

And that's what God did. He made His selection and sent Samuel out to anoint the man as Israel's next king.

God's candidate, however, was so unexpected that no one could believe it. And that's why we need to pay careful attention to this choice the Lord made. By selecting David, the Lord shows us the kind of person He's looking for.

God knew very well that a giant awaited Israel in its near future. And that intimidator would need an exterminator. It would take the right kind of man to pull it off.

But not the one anybody expected.

THE PERSON GOD *Uses*

Have you ever wanted to be used by God? Here's the good news: The Lord is actively, aggressively searching for people to put to work for His eternal purposes *today*. In Ezekiel 22:30, God says, "I sought for a man among them who would make a wall, and stand in the gap before Me on behalf of the land, that I should not destroy it; but I found no one."

Then in 2 Chronicles 16:9 we are reminded, "The eyes of the LORD run to and fro throughout the whole earth, to show Himself strong on behalf of those whose heart is loyal to Him."

God is looking for a person. He's searching nonstop for a man or woman to stand in the gap, to be His representative. And God found such an individual in David.

Can He find it in you?

David was still a teenager as our story begins, but one with seemingly limitless potential. The Lord tapped his servant Samuel on the shoulder and sent him out to anoint the young man as Saul's successor.

> The Lord said to Samuel, "You have mourned long enough for Saul. I have rejected him as king of Israel. Now fill your horn with olive oil and go to Bethlehem. Find a man named Jesse who lives there, for I have selected one of his sons to be my new king." (1 Samuel 16:1, NLT)

Evidently, Samuel was having a hard time getting over Saul. He'd really taken to that tall young man from the tribe of Benjamin. With his own sons as rebellious and wicked as they were, the old prophet had probably come to think of the young Benjamite as a son. And what a disappointment it was when Saul's seemingly promising kingship exploded like a fireworks rocket—one big colorful flash, dissolving into ashes and drifting smoke.

Finally, God had to tell Samuel in plain terms that Saul was history, and He had already selected His new man. Samuel was to fill up his anointing flask and head for the little town of Bethlehem.

Anoint a new king? That had the man of God just a little bit concerned. Let's pick up the biblical account again:

But Samuel asked, "How can I do that? If Saul hears about it, he will kill me." [Notice that Saul had murderous jealousy issues before David ever came on the scene!]

"Take a heifer with you," the LORD replied, "and say that you have come to make a sacrifice to the LORD. Invite Jesse to the sacrifice, and I will show you which of his sons to anoint for me."

So Samuel did as the LORD instructed him. When he arrived at Bethlehem, the leaders of the town became afraid. "What's wrong?" they asked. "Do you come in peace?"

"Yes," Samuel replied. "I have come to sacrifice to the LORD. Purify yourselves and come with me to the sacrifice." Then Samuel performed the purification rite for Jesse and his sons and invited them, too. (vv. 2-5, NLT)

Have you ever tried to unfold one of those big roadmaps inside a car? That's not so bad. The trick is trying to fold it back again! The Lord opened just one panel of His roadmap to Samuel. He told him to go to Bethlehem and that this new king would come from Jesse's family, one of this sheep rancher's sons.

But God didn't tell him which one. Not yet.

That's the way it is with us, too. God unfolds our lives just one panel at a time. We want to see more. We want to unfold the whole map, and see where the road goes, how far it goes, and all the mountains and obstacles that might be waiting for us up ahead. But God shows us just enough to take the next step. He wants us to trust Him for the days ahead, not try to plot our own route through life.

ONE STEP AT A *Time*

Samuel knew a little about this mission God had sent him on. Not as much as he wanted to know, most likely, but enough to get things rolling.

As I look back over my own life, I can't remember a single time God has ever given me a detailed blueprint of all that I was to do. I may have had a sense of what was coming, but I had no idea of when it would happen or where it would happen or how it would happen. I would take one step and then he would show me the next one and the next one. Or he'd have me wait for a while between steps, staying tuned to His frequency for further instructions. The truth is, God's way becomes plain when we start walking in it. Obedience to revealed truth guarantees guidance in matters yet to be revealed.

Remember when the Lord spoke to Philip in the book of Acts? The basic message that time was, "Go to the desert."

That was it.

No GPS coordinates. No itinerary. No expense account. Just, "Hit the road for the desert. Now." And by the way, Philip hadn't exactly been cooling his heels in Jerusalem at the time of that summons. As a matter of fact, he was neck deep in a rip-roarin' revival over in

Samaria. Demons were coming out of people, miracles were taking place, and all kinds of people were coming to faith.

And the Lord said, "Up from here, Philip. Go to the desert."

He didn't say go to the desert and you're going to see some guy from Ethiopia reading out loud from Isaiah 53, so you'd better bone up on that passage and be prepared. God didn't tell him any of that. He just sent him off into the boondocks.

If I'm Philip, I'm asking the Lord, "Why in the world would I want to do that? Do You want me to preach to the cactus or the lizards? Get somebody else. Tap one of the other apostles on the shoulder. Can't You see I'm busy here? Can't you see I'm doing Your work?"

But there's no record that Philip said anything of the kind. When God said, "Go," Philip just up and went. This man's heart was in the right place. He took himself into the desert, *and after he got there*, after he'd taken that first confusing, perplexing step of obedience and faith, then it became clear what he was to do next.

Has God asked you to do something? You're saying, "Oh Lord, reveal Your will to me. What is Your plan for my life?" And you're looking for some great, grandiose blueprint of the next twenty years. But listen carefully. God may already be speaking to you. He may be saying something like, "Why don't you walk across the street and start a conversation with your neighbor. Watch for openings to tell him about your relationship with Me."

"Well that's interesting," you reply, "but I want to reach the world for You, Lord!"

"That's fine. That's good. But right now, I want you to start with your neighbor. See, he's out front right now hosing down his driveway. He's ready to listen. Perfect time."

"But Lord, I want to do great things for You."

"How about doing a few small things for Me first? How about doing the thing that I just set before you?"

There may be a number of little things that God's Spirit leads us to do. Maybe apologizing to someone you've had a conflict with. Or giving some money to someone in your church struggling to make ends meet. Or repaying a debt you've owed for a while. He tells us what He wants done, and we don't want to do it. Then we wonder why "God isn't revealing His will to me." But we need to understand that the *Lord's way becomes plain when we do the next thing we know to do.* And when it comes time to make a further decision or go another mile down the road, He'll be there to guide you for that step, too.

SAMUEL AND THE *Magnificent* SEVEN

So the great prophet Samuel came into town, and it caused quite a sensation. Now you have to understand that Bethlehem was kind of like Podunk. It wasn't some big, important town. We believers tend to hold it in high regard because our Lord was born there. And so we should. But for all practical purposes, this was an out-of-the-way, backwater kind of place.

Jerusalem was the spiritual capital of the world. Bethlehem was just one of many little villages dotting the hillsides of Judea. That's why Micah the prophet said, "But you, Bethlehem Ephrathah, though you are little among the thousands of Judah, yet out of you shall come forth to Me the One to be Ruler in Israel, whose goings forth are from of old, from everlasting" (Micah 5:2).

"Little among the thousands . . ." Just another wide spot on the road to Jerusalem. A diner and a gas station—that kind of place. So for a man the stature of the legendary Samuel to come to town was a very, very big deal. Within moments of the prophet's arrival, the whole town was abuzz. *The prophet Samuel is here. HERE? When? Why? What's going on? Something must be wrong! Why would the man of God come to our little town?*

Later, after Samuel had announced his intentions and readied the sacrifice, there came Jesse, the rancher, and his seven strapping sons. It was kind of like *Bonanza*— Ben Cartwright riding into Virginia City with Adam, Hoss, and Little Joe riding at his side. Heads must have turned.

"Here come Jesse and the boys."

There was a famous Western many years ago called "The Magnificent Seven." And that's what Samuel might have called these guys as they came striding up to the community sacrifice. Samuel must have looked up at them with speculation in his eyes. After giving the family a quick once-over, he was immediately drawn to Eliab—the brother we might call the pick of the litter.

> So it was, when they came, that [Samuel] looked at Eliab and said, "Surely the LORD's anointed is before Him!" But the LORD said to Samuel, "Do not look at his appearance or at his physical stature, because I have refused him. For the LORD does not see as man sees; for man looks at the outward appearance, but the LORD looks at the heart." 1 Samuel 16:6-7

What a fascinating story! Jesse and the Magnificent Seven, led by Eliab, who stood a little taller than all the rest. He was a well-built, good-looking kid, and Samuel was immediately drawn to him. Why? Possibly because Eliab reminded him of Saul. *Oh yeah, this is the one. Look at that guy. He's just got "the look." That kingly bearing. He's got it going. He's gotta be the one.*

But Eliab wasn't the one.

God said no, with a pointed reminder to His prophet not to judge by outward appearances. "I look right past all that exterior stuff," the Lord told Samuel. "I've got My eye on the heart."

It's the same way with us, whether we want to admit it or not. We can be so drawn to beauty and charisma and popularity that we forget all about character. The Lord wanted to teach the prophet—and all the rest of us—an important lesson.

"The LORD, said to Samuel, . . . 'The LORD doesn't make decisions the way you do.'" (1 Samuel 16:7, NLT). And that is true. We judge by looks and clothing, nice hair or white teeth, a muscular build or a great figure. We're all about judging people from the outside in. But God evaluates the other way around; He sees from the inside out. The Lord takes note of a man or woman's motives, intentions, and all of those other qualities mostly hidden from human sight.

So if Eliab wasn't the candidate, who was?

> So Jesse called Abinadab, and made him pass before Samuel. And he said, "Neither has the LORD chosen this one." Then Jesse made Shammah pass by. And he said, "Neither has the LORD chosen this one." Thus Jesse made seven of his sons pass before Samuel. And Samuel said to Jesse, "The LORD has not chosen these." (vv. 8-10)

After the Lord rejected all seven of Jesse's sons, Samuel had a problem. You can almost hear him say under his breath, *"Now* what?"

He turned to Jesse and said, "Is this it? Don't you have any other sons?" The rancher's reply was significant: "There remains yet the youngest, and there he is, keeping the sheep" (v. 11). Out yonder at a distance, little more than a speck on the horizon, there was David, leaning on his shepherd's staff, watching his dad's flock of woolies, humming a little tune, and minding his own business.

The word that Jesse used here for "the youngest" doesn't just mean that David was less in years than the others. It also means that he was least in his father's estimation. So much so that Jesse wouldn't have even included him in an important community occasion like this, if the prophet hadn't specifically asked.

It's sad when a parent disowns or ignores a child or shows favoritism to one over another. And it happens so often. You can read the story of Isaac and Rebekah in the book of Genesis. They both favored a different child. Isaac took a liking to Esau, because Esau would go out in the field and bring back some of that delicious barbecued venison that Isaac loved so much. Rebekah, however, favored Jacob. So this pitted these two boys against each other. And even after the parents were long gone, those boys had a rivalry that carried on into their adult years— and touched their descendents for generations to come.

It reminds us as parents to be evenhanded in the treatment of our sons and daughters, and to remember that each one of our children is unique, with a different bent. Some may be more academic. Some might be more athletic. Some have skills in one area, others have gifting in another. Some are early bloomers, some come into their own after years have gone by. Don't compare your children to one another. *Why can't you be more diligent in your homework like your sister? Why aren't you interested in sports like your brother? Why can't you do this right or that right?* You have to find each child's individual abilities and talents, and then affirm, love, guide, and help them reach their potential as they come to know and then serve the Lord.

In the story of David, this young man's dad wouldn't even acknowledge him. And don't you think David was aware of that?

Maybe that describes you. Maybe your father or mother favored a sibling over you. Or worse yet, they just ignored you. Or neglected to talk to you. Or had a hard time expressing affection. To this day you wonder, *Does my mother even love me? Does my father care about me and what happens to me?*

I trust that they do, but even if perchance they don't, know this: You have a heavenly Father who loves you and takes great pride and delight in you. That's what you need to remember. Those who are rejected of men often become beloved of the Lord. David himself wrote, "When my father and my mother forsake me, then the LORD will take care of me" (Psalm 27:10).

Alan Redpath wrote a wonderful little book on the life of David called *The Making of a Man of God*. And he makes this statement about this aspect of David's life. "The thought of God toward you began before He ever flung a star into space. Then He wrote your name in His heart. It was graven in the palm of His hands before the sky was stretched out in the heavens." [1]

The point is, God knows about your relationship with your parents, and the heartache or disappointment they may have caused you. He knows and He cares. And you need to turn to Him with your pain and disappointment and draw your comfort from His great heart.

A SURPRISE *Choice*

Each of the Magnificent Seven had their moment in the sun before Samuel. You can imagine him squinting his eyes and maybe tilting his head this way and that, listening for the voice of God's Spirit.

And the Lord said, "None of these guys make the cut."

That's when Jesse reluctantly told the prophet about David, and Samuel said, "Send for him. *Nobody eats a bite until he gets here.*" (And that probably didn't endear David to his brothers, either.)

> So [Jesse] sent and brought him in. Now [David] was ruddy, with bright eyes, and good-looking. And the LORD said, "Arise, anoint him; for this is the one!" Then Samuel took the horn of oil and anointed him in the midst of his brothers; and the Spirit of the LORD came upon David from that day forward. So Samuel arose and went to Ramah. (1 Samuel 16:12-13)

Finally, reluctantly, David was summoned from the distant field. "Hey, kid, they want you in town. The prophet Samuel is asking for you, so shake a leg." So David came bounding in, most likely smelling like the sheep he'd been keeping company with for so long.

When you and I think of shepherds in Scripture, we have a pretty favorable impression. Maybe we can remember pictures of shepherds and sheep from our Sunday school classes, or we've seen them in Christian bookstores. Our kids dress up as shepherds in Christmas pageants. Moses had been a shepherd. Jacob and his sons were shepherds. David was a shepherd. The heavenly choir announced the birth of Jesus to shepherds keeping watch over their flocks by night.

But in those days, in that culture, shepherds weren't held in such high regard. Did you know that the testimony of a shepherd wasn't even allowed in a court of law? They were looked down upon. Scorned. If you were having a party or a barbeque, you wouldn't invite any shepherds if there was any way around it.

And David was a shepherd—a young shepherd at that.

He had a job nobody else really wanted. At that time, when he came walking in from the outer pasture, he was a very young man with reddish hair, bursting with youthful enthusiasm.

And God said to Samuel, "That's My boy. Get up and anoint him right now."

Samuel must have been in shock. *Lord, are You joking with me? This red-haired kid? You're turning down Eliab and the rest of the Magnificent Seven for him?* But Samuel knew his God. And he certainly knew better than to question the Lord's decisions or drag his feet about obeying. So he walked over to David, had him kneel, and poured the anointing oil over the young man's head.

Can you imagine what everyone thought? *That old prophet has finally gone senile. Has he lost his mind? There's no way David could be the next king.*

I really don't know if the people present at that feast

fully understood the significance of what was happening in that moment, but it was clear to David. Samuel, too. And for the time being, maybe that's all that mattered.

The Lord obviously knew what He was doing. David was God's choice, and God sees things differently than we do. His brothers and father saw the runt of the litter, a no-account teenager with no future outside of the sheep pasture.

But God saw a giant-killer.

3 | *Characteristics of a* **GIANT-KILLER**

What does a giant-killer look like? Could you pick one out of a crowd? Do you have one in your family? In your church? Do you see one when you look in the mirror each morning? Let's look at some characteristics of a person God can use to cut giants down to size.

#1: GOD USES *Ordinary* PEOPLE

In many ways, David was the polar opposite of King Saul. Saul came from a family where he was loved and valued, and David from a family where he was neglected, belittled, even disliked. Saul had Hollywood handsomeness—star material. David was a relatively ordinary shepherd boy, though good-looking. Saul was attractive on the outside but inside he was vain, shallow, and devoid of true integrity. In contrast, David, though he was young, had a deep spiritual life and an intense devotion to God.

Remember what Paul wrote to the believers in Corinth? "Brothers, think of what you were when you were called. Not many of you were wise by human standards; not many were influential; not many were of noble birth. But God chose the foolish things of the world to shame the wise; God chose the weak things of the world to shame the strong. He chose the lowly things of this world and the despised things—and the things that are not—to nullify the things that are, so that no one may boast before him" (1 Corinthians 1:26-29, NIV).

It's true, isn't it?

But that's hard for us to admit. We don't like to think of ourselves as weak. We like think ourselves strong.

I had the opportunity to be on Larry King Live in 2005, and the subject turned to suffering. Larry asked why it even existed in the first place.

I told Larry that God can use suffering in our lives, often to bring us to faith. I mentioned a C. S. Lewis quote, where he pointed out that God "whispers to us in our pleasures, but shouts to us in our pain."

I then related a story about a lady who had breast cancer, who had come to our church office the previous Sunday morning after the first service. She told me how this tragedy had gotten her attention, and so she was turning to God.

Larry interrupted me and said, "How do you know it's not a crutch? I mean, I've got breast cancer—I've got to pray to *something!* You know, there's a believer in every foxhole."

I responded, "Thank God for that crutch! Larry, He's not a crutch to me, He's a whole hospital!"

Larry smiled, pointed at me, and said, "Good line!" Then he turned to his director and said, "Write that down!"

As we went to commercial break, off camera Larry said to me, "You must use that line a lot." I told him I did occasionally, but it was true. And it is! I wasn't trying to be witty, just truthful. I am not ashamed to admit that I'm weak and I need God. The person who is afraid to admit that is really a fool.

But we forget about that sometimes. We get caught up in the idea that fame and fashion and style and charisma are the most important things in life. We always wish some big-time, important people would get saved. "Man, I wish a movie star would come to Christ. Or a rock star. Or some prominent politician or news anchor person—or someone really well known or impressive. Then we could say, 'So-and-so is on *our* side now.'"

The truth is, God will save anyone who calls upon Him in faith. But in many cases, those who do call are just regular, everyday sorts of people who realize their need for a Savior. These are men and women and boys and girls who may not be the most talented or brilliant people to walk the planet. They may not be bodybuilders or cover girls. They may not be the type to survive six months on *Jeopardy.* They're just people who come to God in their weakness, and say, "Lord, if You can use me, here I am. I'm available." Refusing to rely on human resources, they allow God to work with them and through them in a spectacular, supernatural way.

That's good news for us ordinary people.

And bad news for giants.

We live in a media-driven culture enamored with celebrity. There are people out there who know all the magazines, all the TV shows, all the Tinseltown gossip.

We think, "This person is so charismatic and cool!" Then you see him or her interviewed on TV and you realize, "This person has no mind." If they didn't have lines written for them in a script, they wouldn't be able to put two coherent sentences together. Still, so many admire and adulate these shallow, empty-headed celebrities today. We breathlessly follow their every move, secretly wishing we were living their lives. But I can assure you, God is not impressed.

The Lord sometimes picks men and women for prominent kingdom roles that you and I would never pick! He draws people from the back of the line. He plucks people out of obscurity.

Before he entered into ministry, D. L. Moody once had a man say to him, "Moody, the world has yet to see what God can do in and through a man who is wholly dedicated to Him." Moody thought about it for a moment and replied, "I want to be that man." And God took that shoe salesman and made him into the most powerful evangelist of his era. You might say he went from selling soles to saving souls.

Billy Graham was a dairy farmer, known to the local populace as Billy Frank. And God raised him up to be the greatest evangelist the world has ever seen.

God delights to use commonplace people and do extraordinary works through their lives. It makes sense, doesn't it? When a non-spectacular person ends up doing amazingly spectacular things . . . guess Who gets the glory?

#2: GOD USES *Heart-Hungry* PEOPLE

David was a truly spiritual man. Not some pasted-on, blow-dried, holier-than-thou spirituality. He was the real deal. Genuine through and through. That's what I like about him. When David was upset, he told the Lord all about it. You can see it again and again in the psalms. He talked plainly about how he felt about things, and didn't try to hide it or smooth it over with religious-sounding words. But then a few lines down in the same psalm he would come right back and remind himself of the love and faithfulness of his God. When you read psalms like that, you can relate to this guy. This was a real human being, who put on his sandals one foot at a time.

Many times people think being spiritual means you have to almost be artificial. You can't have fun. You can't enjoy life. You can't laugh at this and you can't smile at that. When I first became a Christian as a high schooler, I signed up for one of Calvary Chapel's summer camps. I had seen Pastor Chuck Smith, the founder of Calvary Chapels, from a distance, but had never met him before. To tell the truth, I was pretty nervous around him.

Then at dinner one night, I found myself seated at his table. In fact, he was sitting right next to me.

Because of my proximity to this great Bible teacher, I was trying to pull off my best imitation of how I thought a "serious" Christian would act. I actually imagined that was what was expected of me. You have to understand a little of my pre-Christian background here. Before I came to Christ, I was the biggest goof-off prankster of all time. A wild and crazy guy.

But now here I was sitting at a dinner table with *Chuck Smith.* I thought to myself, *I'm a Christian now. I have to leave the things of the world behind. There will be no more laughing, no more joking, no more pranks. I will read the Bible and pray and sleep and eat and that's it.*

As the food was being served, I wanted some punch in my glass. So I turned to Pastor Chuck sitting beside me, cleared my throat politely, and said, "Pastor Chuck, could I have some punch, please?"

"Why sure," he said. He took the pitcher and began pouring it in my glass. As he was pouring, I thought to myself, *Pastor Chuck Smith is pouring my punch. It's like . . . anointed punch.*

Pastor Chuck kept pouring. Half full, three-quarters full, almost full, full, *overflowing!* As the punch was splashing over my hand and onto the floor, I was thinking, *What's happening here? Does Pastor Chuck know he's doing this? Is there some spiritual message here? Maybe something about abundance?*

I looked at Chuck. And he started laughing.

He was having fun and shaking me out of my fake spiritual performance. That was a real revelation to me. *I can still have fun and be a Christian! This is good.* And Chuck Smith? Well, I soon found out he didn't walk around with his hands folded and his eyes cast toward heaven. He was human. A very spiritual man, yes, but to this day a man who thoroughly enjoys laughter and life.

A few years later, I had the opportunity to spend time with the famous British author and expositor, Alan Redpath, whom I already quoted. I was a young pastor at this point. One evening I was invited to dinner by my friend Don McClure, who was also a pastor and a long-time friend of Dr. Redpath.

I couldn't believe how blessed I was to be around this wonderful British gentleman and world-renowned Bible teacher. At that point in my life, I regarded Alan Redpath about the same way that I had regarded Chuck Smith when I was a new believer.

This is Alan Redpath the man of God, the revered Bible teacher. When I was around him I was on my best behavior. No goofing around. No laughing. I tried to carry myself with dignity.

Quite frankly, it was phony as a three-dollar bill. I wasn't being myself at all. When he wasn't around, I would relax and cut up and joke about all kinds of things. One night when Dr. Redpath wasn't with us, Pastor Don and I were eating together in a nice restaurant. I took a bite of my food and, for no apparent reason, threw my fork over my shoulder.

"Why did you do that?" Don asked me.

"Aren't these disposable?" I replied. It was just a random bit of craziness, a joke. (You had to be there.) Two nights later, I was sitting at dinner with Dr. Redpath. Eating quietly and thoughtfully, I was trying my very best to remember my etiquette and table manners and ask deeply spiritual questions.

All of a sudden a fork hit me square in the chest.

I looked up. My dinner partner was smiling. I couldn't believe my eyes. The Great British Expositor, Dr. Alan Redpath, had just thrown a fork at me!

"Aren't these disposable?" he asked.

And suddenly we were both laughing out loud. Don had told him what I'd done, and for whatever reason, Dr. Redpath thought that was funny . . . so he did it to me. This was an even greater revelation to me. I can be a *pastor* and still goof around.

I can remember times of being at Billy and Ruth Graham's house, hanging around with them and watching them enjoy life, laugh, tease each other, and have fun. Just regular, relaxed people like you'd meet in your own church.

The most spiritual people I have ever met—and I've had the opportunity to meet wonderful, godly people all over the world—have always been down-to-earth, normal, real people. You can spot phony, tacked-on spirituality a mile away, and the truth is, it's not spirituality at all.

It's just an act. And God isn't impressed with that one bit.

David was authentic. If you want to really see who this man was and what made him tick, just read the psalms. It's all there for you, a realistic portrait of his life.

In Psalm 57:7 (AMP), David wrote: "My heart is fixed O LORD . . ." What was it fixed on? David's whole life was focused on the Lord. He wasn't fickle. His objective—the overpowering desire of his heart—was clear. In fact, in Psalm 27:4 (AMP) he said, "One thing have I asked of the Lord, that will I seek: that I may dwell in the house of the Lord all the days of my life, to behold and gaze upon the beauty of the Lord and to inquire in His temple."

David knew where he was going in life, and one thing was more important to him than anything else: to be as close to God as he could possibly be, in the dwelling place of the Lord.

Many of us feel that way. We love being at church. We love the worship. We love the Bible study and prayer. We love seeing God work. And after the service, we like to kick back and just spend time with each other. We develop friendships and relationships. We're all inter-twined.

That's what it's all about! It's a community. The Holy Spirit gives us that strong desire to be with God's people, and sometimes we just can't get enough of it. We've come to know the value of fellowship.

David longed to "dwell in the house of the LORD" and to "behold His beauty in the temple." Back in the old covenant, the Temple—preceded by the Tabernacle or the tent—was the place where man would meet God. David was essentially saying, *I wish I could edge as close as I could get the presence of the Lord, and just stay there day and night.* In that Tabernacle or Temple was the inner sanctum, the holy of holies, where only the high priest could enter.

Yet today as Christians, we can enter into "the holy of holies" 24 hours a day, 365 days a year. Hebrews 10:19 says, "Brothers, since we have confidence to enter the Most Holy Place by the blood of Jesus, by a new and living way opened for us through the curtain, that is, his body, and since we have a great priest over the house of God, let us draw near to God with a sincere heart in full assurance of faith." (NIV) The good news is that you don't have to be in the building—"the temple"—to enjoy the presence of the Lord.

If you're stuck on the commute every day, out on the freeway driving for an hour and a half or two hours, you can make your car into a sanctuary! Put on some praise music. Pop in a Bible teaching tape or CD. Tune in to a Christian radio station. Listen to the Bible on CD. Your car can be a temple of worship to the Lord.

You don't have to be on your cell phone all the time, like 90 percent of the people I see on the freeway. *Who are these people talking to?* Everyone is on cell phones now. Have you noticed that? Babies have cell phones. Dogs have cell phones. Everywhere I look everyone is talking into these little bitty phones or headsets.

Turn the cell phone off for a few minutes. You'll survive. You can probably make it for a full hour without having a conversation with another person.

How about having a conversation with the Lord?

You don't need to distract yourself from driving by punching in His number—possibly rear-ending the car in front of you. Just start talking to Him. He's always on the line. Spend some time in His presence, and worship Him. But you have to be a little careful. You probably shouldn't lift up your hands while you're worshipping on the freeway—it's best to keep your hands on the wheel. Even so, you can keep company with the mighty God of the universe who loves you, and it will make all the difference in your day.

That's what David wanted. *One thing in life.* He was an ordinary man and a spiritual man.

#3: GOD USES *Faithful* PEOPLE

At this particular time in David's life, his primary responsibility was caring for the family flock. No doubt he would spend long hours meditating on Scripture, writing music, and worshipping the Lord. It was there that the Lord gave him some enduring truths like Psalm 23. "The LORD is my shepherd; I shall not want. He makes me to lie down in green pastures; He leads me beside the still waters. He restores my soul . . . . Yea, though I walk through the valley of the shadow of death, I will fear no evil; for You are with me . . . ."

As He would tend and protect his sheep, he thought about how the Lord tended and protected him.

Although David couldn't have realized it at the time, God was preparing him. I don't know that this young man had any clue of what was ahead. But the Lord did. And before David could reach the level of greatness God intended for him, there were tests to pass. I think one of those tests was simply to faithfully watch his flock of sheep. Another test was to courageously protect that flock from dangerous predators. And he passed every test.

Many times—perhaps most of the time—you and I don't even know when we're being tested. We don't realize it, but God is prepping us for something greater. He is getting you ready today for something He intends to do in your life tomorrow. So stay faithful where He has placed you. Walk with Him day by day. You might be in the middle of a test right now, without even knowing it.

Sometimes the tests are obvious—and big. Sometimes they're very small, and not so obvious at all. Tests of integrity. Tests of honesty. Tests of faithfulness. David was faithful to the Lord in the small tests, so that when the big tests came, as we will see, He was ready.

But it was a strange thing. Israel's leader and mightiest prophet had anointed him with oil in front of his family and his community. No one who had his eyes open could have missed the significance of that action. When a prophet like Samuel anointed a man, he was destined for the throne.

But do you know what happened next?

Nothing.

At least as far as the human eye could see, nothing changed at all. Samuel returned to Ramah. David went back to his sheep. His father and his brothers returned home. King Saul remained on his throne.

David, son of Jesse, had been anointed. But everything just went on as usual. David had gone through that awesome experience of being chosen by God . . . but he just kept on with what he had been doing. He may have been anointed king, but God hadn't told him what came next.

How could he know that what came next was a giant?

If David had been expecting a lot of rapid-fire changes in his life or his routine, he was going to be a little let down. Because he had a long wait in front of him.

In his excellent book on the life of David, Chuck Swindoll makes this statement. "David didn't go down to the department store and try on crowns. He didn't order a new set of business cards telling the printer, 'Change it from shepherd to king elect.' He didn't have a badge saying I am the new man. He didn't go have a new chariot shined up for him and go running through the streets of Bethlehem yelling, 'I am God's choice. You are looking at Saul's replacement.' " [2]

David just waited for further orders.

And then, seemingly out of the blue, those orders came.

But the Spirit of the LORD departed from Saul, and a distressing spirit from the LORD troubled him. And

Saul's servants said to him, "Surely, a distressing spirit from God is troubling you. Let our master now command your servants, who are before you, to seek out a man who is a skillful player on the harp. And it shall be that he will play it with his hand when the distressing spirit from God is upon you, and you shall be well."

So Saul said to his servants, "Provide me now a man who can play well, and bring him to me."

Then one of the servants answered and said, "Look, I have seen a son of Jesse the Bethlehemite, who is skillful in playing, a mighty man of valor, a man of war, prudent in speech, and a handsome person; and the LORD is with him."

Therefore Saul sent messengers to Jesse, and said, "Send me your son David, who is with the sheep." And Jesse took a donkey loaded with bread, a skin of wine, and a young goat, and sent them by his son David to Saul. So David came to Saul and stood before him. And he loved him greatly, and he became his armor-bearer. Then Saul sent to Jesse, saying, "Please let David stand before me, for he has found favor in my sight." And so it was, whenever the spirit from God was upon Saul, that David would take a harp and play it with his hand. Then Saul would become refreshed and well, and the distressing spirit would depart from him. (1 Samuel 16:14-23)

In God's sovereignty and perfect timing, David's ascent to the throne coincided with Saul's slow and pain-

ful descent from the throne. Without God's empower-
ing Holy Spirit in his life, Saul was no longer effectively
ruling as king of Israel. God had wanted Saul to succeed,
but Saul sinned against the Lord over and over again,
constantly pushing the envelope.

On one occasion he went too far. God had told him to
utterly destroy a sworn and deadly enemy of Israel—and
all of their animals as well—and Saul had failed to do so.
When confronted by the prophet Samuel, he lied about
what he had done, and said he had kept back animals he'd
been commanded to destroy because he "wanted to offer
them to the Lord as a sacrifice."

The prophet's reply to that lame excuse was classic:
"What is more pleasing to the LORD: your burnt offerings
and sacrifices or your obedience to his voice? Obedience
is far better than sacrifice. Listening to him is much
better than offering the fat of rams. Rebellion is as bad
as the sin of witchcraft, and stubbornness is as bad as
worshiping idols. So because you have rejected the word
of the LORD, he has rejected you from being king"
(1 Samuel 15:22-23, NLT).

What terrible words to hear! Saul forsook God, and God
forsook Saul. Disobeying God is serious business. Yes, we
have a loving, forgiving, kind, and gracious God. But we can
never afford to be careless about obedience to His Word.
God takes disobedience very, very seriously. Paul wrote to
Timothy, "If we endure, we shall also reign with Him. If
we deny Him, He also will deny us" (2 Timothy 2:12).

By the time Saul's servants found David to play the harp for the king, Saul was already feeling the effects of his break from the Lord. The Bible tells us that "a distressing spirit" was sent to him from God. What's that all about? Just this: God in His sovereignty allowed an evil spirit to torment Saul. The Lord was saying in effect, "I am going to punish you for presuming upon the office of king of My people. I have told you you're done, the throne no longer belongs to you. But you refuse to give up."

We have to remember that this story takes place in the Old Testament, under the old covenant before Christ. Saul, in my opinion, was never a true believer. He went through the motions for a while, but pretty much threw his life away. After a good beginning, it didn't take long for his dark side to emerge. He became a violent, evil man, eaten alive by jealousy, and a rebel against the Lord. For more on the life of this unusual character, I recommend you read my book, *Losers and Winners, Saints and Sinners.* I have a whole chapter on this wayward king.

We have to understand that when we come into the new covenant and become Christians, with Christ living inside of us, we don't have to fear distressing spirits overtaking us. We can certainly be oppressed by demonic powers, we can be attacked on the outside. But we cannot be possessed on the inside. Jesus is not into a timeshare arrangement with the devil. When He takes residence in a human heart, He is the sole occupant.

In Saul, we're dealing with a man who never was a believer to begin with, a man who had repeatedly hardened his heart against God, and rejected the work of the Spirit in his life. So the Lord allowed a distressing spirit to come and torment him. He did not have that hedge of protection around him that God gave to Job and others.

Yet isn't it interesting? When David sat before the king and played music as unto the Lord, it had a soothing, calming effect on Saul. The demons didn't like the praise music, and they retreated. And by the way, they still don't like it.

Known for his musical skills, David was summoned into the king's service. It's clear to me that Saul had no idea David had been anointed as king at this point. Otherwise, this would have been a short little jam session for David.

But God was already working things out, moving the chess pieces into position behind the scenes. It's something He loves to do as we yield our lives to Him and seek to be obedient to the voice of His Spirit.

#4: GOD USES *Faithful* PEOPLE

Why was David summoned to such a high place in the kingdom at such a young age? He had a good reputation. Look again at 1 Samuel 16:18 "The son of Jesse is a talented harp player. Not only that; he is brave and strong and has good judgment. He is also a fine-looking young man, and the LORD is with him" (NLT).

Do you have a good reputation? Does your reputation precede you? If someone were to ask someone you know about you, how would that person answer? How would he or she describe you?

David had a godly reputation. Everybody knew he had a special walk with God, and that God's favor was all over him. Do people know that about you? If you want to be a leader, if you want to be used by God, the Bible says you need good character and standing. In speaking about the qualifications of an elder in 1 Timothy 3:6-7, Paul writes, "He must not be a recent convert, or he may become conceited and fall under the same judgment as the devil. He must also have a good reputation with outsiders, so that he will not fall into disgrace and into the devil's trap" (NIV).

David was ready now. God had tested and tried him, and he had come through those tests. Now he is invited into the king's presence.

Notice that this young man made no attempt to pull rank. He didn't say or even imply, "By the way, Saul, you're on your way out and I'm on my way in." He just faithfully did what God had set before him. He did his job, and waited on the Lord for the next thing, the next instruction from heaven. What a great way to live!

1 Samuel 16:21 says, "David came to Saul and stood before him." Or literally, attended to him. Whenever that demon would begin to torment Saul, David was summoned and he would play a stringed instrument. I

think he probably sang to the Lord as well, and Saul would become refreshed and find release—at least temporarily—from the oppression. Another translation says, "This eased Saul." Still another version renders it, "He played for Saul till Saul breathed freely."

It seems to me that someone who really cared about the king would have said, "Saul, you need to get things right with God. You need to call for the prophet Samuel and do some repenting."

But no one said that. Maybe they were afraid of him. The best they could do was advise him to bring someone in with a little music to soothe his tortured soul. When David played, the demon left Saul alone for a while, and he had a little peace. It could have been better, but it was at least something.

There are people like this today. They're facing some trial or heartbreak in life, and they say to themselves, *I'd better get to church.* They'll find some Christian they know and say, "Let me come to church with you." And they'll start coming for a few weeks. Maybe a month or two. And they like it! They begin to get a taste of what it's like to live a truly spiritual life. They drink in the music, the joy, and the teaching from God's Word. They realize that there is something real and genuine going on around them, and they sense God's love and peace in that place.

But then, as soon as their problem goes away or recedes to the background, they go right back to their old ways again. They never really change at all. Sure, they enjoyed the ambiance . . . but they never believed. They never stepped out in faith to receive what God had for them.

Saul was content to listen to David's praise music, but that's all of God he really wanted.

David could very easily have resented or been impatient with the role of court musician. He could have said, "I've been anointed as Israel's king. Why am I sitting on a stool playing the harp? I'm not the king's personal musician. I want to ascend to the throne." But David was content to wait for the Lord's timing. In the meantime, he used his God-given gifts and did the thing that was set before him. He was faithful.

But no one is home free after passing one test. Life on this side of heaven is full of tests, one after another. And the next one on the horizon for David was very, very large. In fact, it was giant.

4 │ *Facing Down*
a **GIANT**

The Philistines now mustered their army for battle and camped between Socoh in Judah and Azekah at Ephes-dammim. Saul countered by gathering his troops near the valley of Elah. So the Philistines and Israelites faced each other on opposite hills, with the valley between them.

Then Goliath, a Philistine champion from Gath, came out of the Philistine ranks to face the forces of Israel. He was a giant of a man, measuring over nine feet tall! He wore a bronze helmet and a coat of mail that weighed 125 pounds. He also wore bronze leggings, and he slung a bronze javelin over his back. The shaft of his spear was as heavy and thick as a weaver's beam, tipped with an iron spearhead that weighed fifteen pounds. An armor bearer walked ahead of him carrying a huge shield.

Goliath stood and shouted across to the Israelites, "Do you need a whole army to settle this? Choose someone to fight for you, and I will represent the Philistines. We will settle this dispute in single combat! If your man is able to kill me, then we will be your slaves. But if I kill him, you will be our slaves! I defy the armies of Israel!

Send me a man who will fight with me!" When Saul and the Israelites heard this, they were terrified and deeply shaken. (1 Samuel 17:1-11, NLT)

Divine opportunities usually (if not always) arrive unexpectedly.

For David, it started with a simple errand. His dad had said to him, "David, your brothers are out there serving on the front lines, fighting the Philistines. I want you to take some bread and cheese to them. Make sure they're okay."

David said, "Yes, sir," tucked the cheese sandwiches into a bag, and set off immediately.

There is no record that Jesse said, "By the way, son, there's a nine-foot plus champion over there named Goliath. While you're delivering the food to your brothers, I want you to take him out and chop off his head."

Who would have ever thought or imagined such a thing? This was just a simple delivery—like a pizza run. As a spiritual man and a faithful man, David followed through and did what his father asked.

In the course of that simple little duty, however, he came upon an amazing scene—and the opportunity of a lifetime.

That's the way it usually works. Life is something that happens on your way to somewhere else. Challenges and opportunities arise out of our normal rounds, while we're doing our normal things. As we're being faithful to be what God has called us to be and do what He has called us to do, doors will unexpectedly open before us. That's why it's so very important to walk in the Spirit every day of our lives, and to be ready for whatever God brings across our path.

When David arrived at the battlefront, he could hardly believe his eyes. Here was this oversized Philistine belching out a challenge to the armies of Israel. Taunts and blasphemies poured from his mouth, but what was even more amazing to David was that *no one was lifting a finger to do anything about it.*

You'd have to be just a little awe-inspired when faced with this massive freak of nature. Goliath had on a suit of armor strapped onto a nine-foot-six-inch frame. The armor alone weighed almost 200 pounds—not counting a bronze helmet the size of a washtub and a huge javelin with a head that weighed 25 pounds.

The Philistine had posed his mocking challenge of single combat to Saul and the Israelites for forty days running—twice a day—and the army sank deeper and deeper into despair. Goliath had them psyched out without ever lifting a finger in battle. He had already beaten them down and defeated them.

But not everyone.

There was someone new in camp. A red-headed young stranger with a bag of bread and cheese. David heard the noise and commotion, and quickly made his way to the battle line to see what was up.

And he was awestruck. Not because of the Philistine giant, but because this enemy was blaspheming God and no one was responding.

That made David angry. Very angry. And it was good that he felt this indignation.

Did you know you can get mad in a good way? You can get royally angry—righteously indignant—and not be in sin. Paul writes: "In your anger do not sin: Do not let the sun go down while you are still angry" (Ephesians 4:26, NIV). In other words, don't let the anger take possession of you or push you into behavior that displeases the Lord. But David's anger at the situation confronting Israel in that moment was the right kind of anger. And it was about to move him to action.

This isn't right. This shouldn't be. This man should not be blaspheming the God of Israel. Why doesn't somebody shut him up?

No sooner did David speak up about the situation, however, than he ran into opposition. From whom? The enemy? No. Interestingly, it was his own big brother Eliab, the Golden Boy, who laid into him with a vengeance.

> But when David's oldest brother, Eliab, heard David talking to the men, he was angry. "What are you doing around here anyway?" he demanded. "What about those few sheep you're supposed to be taking care of? I know about your pride and dishonesty. You just want to see the battle!"

"What have I done now?" David replied. "I was only
asking a question!" (1 Samuel 12: 28-29, NLT)

"What's the matter, little boy?" Eliab sneers. "Tired of
being at home? Come down to watch the big boys? What
are you even doing here? I know your arrogance. I know
your pride. Why don't you go back to your tiny little flock
of smelly sheep and leave us alone."

David just ignored his older brother's mockery and
asked for an audience with King Saul.

It's one thing when we find ourselves opposed by the
non-believing world for seeking to serve the Lord, but it's
a whole different matter when our own Christian brothers and sisters turn on us. It is amazing to me how we in
the church can often quibble and argue over the small-
est matters, while millions grope in the darkness and
millions more slip into hell.

One of the biggest challenges we face when we go into
a community to hold one of our evangelistic events is
simply getting the local churches to work together. You
can't believe what a big task that is. In some places it's
like the idea of working together is a novelty, something
they'd never thought to try. And do you know where it has
to start? With pastors. First we have to get pastors to talk
to fellow pastors. And many times they don't! They have
virtually no communication with other church leaders
in their community. After we find a way to bring them
together, then we want to get them to pray and eventually
work side by side with their fellow area pastors.

How often we see believers opposing believers. You step out there in faith and try to do something for the Lord, and the voices of the critics start rolling in.

"You shouldn't do that."

"That's crazy. The Lord could never bless that."

"You won't succeed. This is going to be a big failure."

"You're just doing this in the flesh."

Let me just say this, my friend. If you've ever gone out and tried something for the Lord and failed, you have my thanks. I really mean that. Thank you for failing.

"But Greg," you protest. "Shouldn't we be successful?"

The truth is, the doorway to success is most often entered through the hallway of failure. You show me anybody who has succeeded in any ministry or endeavor for the Lord, and I will guarantee there was a string of failures that preceded it. They didn't get it quite right. They got it a little wrong. They had to go back to the drawing table. But thank God they at least tried! How much better to be the person who steps out for the Lord and runs into failure than to be a complacent critic who plays it safe and does nothing, who won't take a step of faith, who won't say, "Let's see what the Lord will do."

In this story, it was brother Eliab, that big handsome son of Jesse that Samuel thought would make such a great king, who was ripping David up one side and down the other. But David didn't let it deter him. He pressed on and got his audience with Saul. He wanted to hear for himself why the army of Israel was paralyzed before that arrogant braggart of a Philistine.

> Then David said to Saul, "Let no man's heart fail because of him; your servant will go and fight with this Philistine."

> And Saul said to David, "You are not able to go against this Philistine to fight with him; for you are a youth, and he a man of war from his youth."

> But David said to Saul, "Your servant used to keep his father's sheep, and when a lion or a bear came and took a lamb out of the flock, I went out after it and struck it, and delivered the lamb from its mouth; and when it arose against me, I caught it by its beard, and struck and killed it. Your servant has killed both lion and bear; and this uncircumcised Philistine will be like one of them, seeing he has defied the armies of the living God. . . . The LORD, who delivered me from the paw of the lion and from the paw of the bear, He will deliver me from the hand of this Philistine."

> And Saul said to David, "Go, and the LORD be with you!" (1 Samuel 17: 32-37)

Saul must have been somewhat amused when David came to talk to him about taking on Goliath. You and what army, kid? You're hardly more than a boy, and you're going to face off with a nine-foot-six-inch monster who's been a warrior from his youth?

Frankly, it should have been Saul himself who stepped out to face Goliath. After all, he stood taller than all the other Israelites—not to even mention he was the King! He would have been a worthy opponent. But he was afraid—and paralyzed—along with everyone else.

Maybe King Saul thought Goliath would take one look at David and laugh himself to death. At the very least, Saul might have thought, this should be amusing.

Saul told him, "If you're determined to do this thing, you'd better try on my armor." That made the scene even more comical. David clanked around in that big, heavy armor, and said, in effect, "No way. I can't hardly even walk in this stuff. I'll just go out there and trust the Lord."

"Well, go for it, David," Saul tells him. "And God bless you. (You'll need it, son!)"

In David's mind, however, the battle was already won. It was already a done deal, and Goliath was history.

Where did this teenager find such boldness? We find the key in verses 35 through 37. Describing his protection of the sheep against predators, David declared, "If the animal turns on me, I catch it by the jaw and club it to death. I have done this to both lions and bears, and I'll do it to this pagan Philistine, too, for he has defied the armies of the living God! The LORD who saved me from the claws of the lion and the bear will save me from this Philistine!" (NLT).

That's what we need to remember: The battle is the Lord's. Why do we find ourselves defeated so often by the giants in our life? It's a simple answer: Because we try to face them in our own strength, and we fail.

This brings us to our first principle in how to deal with giants.

PRINCIPLE #1: ACT ON *Faith and Trust* GOD

He picked up five smooth stones from a stream and put them in his shepherd's bag. Then, armed only with his shepherd's staff and sling, he started across to fight Goliath.

Goliath walked out toward David with his shield bearer ahead of him, sneering in contempt at this ruddy-faced boy. "Am I a dog," he roared at David, "that you come at me with a stick?" And he cursed David by the names of his gods. "Come over here, and I'll give your flesh to the birds and wild animals!" Goliath yelled.

David shouted in reply, "You come to me with sword, spear, and javelin, but I come to you in the name of the Lord Almighty—the God of the armies of Israel, whom you have defied. Today the Lord will conquer you, and I will kill you and cut off your head. And then I will give the dead bodies of your men to the birds and wild animals, and the whole world will know that there is a God in Israel! And everyone will know that the Lord does not need weapons to rescue his people. It is his battle, not ours. The Lord will give you to us!"

As Goliath moved closer to attack, David quickly ran out to meet him. Reaching into his shepherd's bag and taking out a stone, he hurled it from his sling and hit the Philistine in the forehead. The stone sank in, and Goliath stumbled and fell face downward to the ground. So David triumphed over the Philistine giant with only a stone and sling. And since he had no sword, he ran over and pulled Goliath's sword from its sheath. David used it to kill the giant and cut off his head.

When the Philistines saw that their champion was dead, they turned and ran. Then the Israelites gave a great shout of triumph and rushed after the Philistines, chasing them as far as Gath and the gates of Ekron. The bodies of the dead and wounded Philistines were strewn all along the road from Shaaraim, as far as Gath and Ekron. (1 Samuel 17:40-52, NLT)

What a story! No matter how many times you've heard it or read it, it makes your heart beat a little faster. What a victory this was for David—invigorating all of Israel. Like ripples spreading outward from a stone tossed into a still pond, David's faith and courage swept through the whole army, changing them from cringing cowards to the courageous warriors God intended them to be.

And the Philistines? *They* became the cringing cowards, throwing down their weapons and running like scared rabbits. The will and the pride of the enemy had been broken.

Where did it all start? It started with a young man who stepped out of the safety zone and was willing to take a chance and trust God.

What about the giants we face in our own lives right now? As we've already noted, you may have something that looms large and seemingly undefeatable in your life. After enduring failure after failure, you've come to the place where you believe that giant will just always be there. It will be a big, ugly, humiliating part of your land-scape from now on. In that sense, you've come to accept the giant.

That was the problem with the Israelites. Goliath had become a part of their lives. For forty days he had lumbered up to the battle line to shout his challenge and his mockery. In Scripture, forty is always the number of testing. Twice each day he snarled insults and blasphemy at Israel's finest soldiers. After all those days, they'd gotten used to it. They could set their watch by it.

Maybe that's what has happened with you and your giant. You've started thinking, "This is just a part of my life. I don't want it. I don't like it. But I've gotten used to it. It's always going to be there."

No! You must be willing to accept that this giant can and by the grace of God will fall. But it will mean climb-ing out of that foxhole and stepping out to the battle line to face that thing. It will mean taking a chance and putting your faith in God as never before.

PRINCIPLE #2: REMEMBER THAT
the Battle **IS THE LORD'S**

David had shouted at the enemy, "This is *His* battle, not ours. The Lord will give you to us!"

In Ephesians 6, Paul reminds us that we are engaged in an ongoing spiritual warfare and we must fight it with spiritual weapons. He goes on to tell us about the shield of faith, the breastplate of righteousness, the sword of the Spirit, and the helmet of salvation.

But before he says a single word about which piece of armor to wear where, the apostle tells us in verse 10: "My brethren, be strong in the Lord and in the power of His might."

Right off the top, Paul is saying, "Before I tell you about armor, you need to hear this. Be strong in the Lord. Stand in His strength. Walk in His strength. Do battle in His strength. Don't depend on yourself. Willpower and human strategies aren't going to get it done. It is dependence upon God that will bring victory. God is going to work through you and give you the strength to live for Him and to obey Him and overcome this giant in your life."

Jesus said, "Apart from me you can do nothing" (John 15:5, NIV). And then Paul adds, "I can do all things through Christ who strengthens me" (Philippians 4:13).

It seems like such a simple lesson.

It seems so obvious.

But again and again and again, it is the very thing that leaves us paralyzed or cowering before the giants in our lives. In your own strength, you're going to lose. Period. End of sentence. But in the power of God, you will prevail.

Let's dig into this just a little deeper. In Ephesians, Paul prays that believers would understand what God had done for them. In chapter 1, verses 19-22, he says,

> "I pray that you will begin to understand the incredible greatness of his power for us who believe him. This is the same mighty power that raised Christ from the dead and seated him in the place of honor at God's right hand in the heavenly realms. Now he is far above any ruler or authority or power or leader or anything else in this world or in the world to come. And God has put all things under the authority of Christ" (NIV).

Okay, you say, it's nice to know that Jesus is there in that position of power. But what does this have to do with me?

Answer: *Everything.*

It has everything to do with taking down every giant that mocks you and bullies you and makes your life miserable. If you're ever going to cut the legs out from under the giants in your life, you have to understand the power that will accomplish that.

Paul continues on then in Ephesians 2:4-6 to tell us that we at this moment are actually seated with Jesus Christ in the heavenly realms, because we are one with Him.

You are seated in the heavenlies. What does that mean? That means that positionally, Christ is above all principality and power, might and dominion, and *you are seated right there with Him, covered by His authority.*

Sometimes you will see a Christian friend and say, "How are you doing?" And he or she will sigh, and answer back, "Oh, I'm all right under the circumstances." *Well what are you doing under those?* You don't need to be "under the circumstances." You need to remember and rehearse what God has done for you. In the deepest of realities, you are already with Christ in heaven and Christ is right here on earth with you. So live in the victory that Jesus has purchased for you! There is no power you have to bend the knee to other than His power. There is no addiction that needs to control your life.

There is no lifestyle you cannot break free from.

Jesus said, "Therefore if the Son makes you free, you shall be free indeed" (John 8:36). So what we need to know is that we cannot fight these giants in our own strength, but we can do it in God's strength.

And we have that strength right now in Jesus Christ.

That is what David understood. The battle wasn't his. It didn't depend on his stature, his armor, his skill, his fighting experience, even his family's blessing. It was the Lord's battle, and the Lord's battles get won.

Remember this . . . the task ahead of us is never as great as the Power behind us.

PRINCIPLE #3: *Attack* YOUR GIANTS

Early in the story we read that the Israelites said "Have you seen this man who has come up?" referring to Goliath (1 Samuel 17:25). In other words, at some point in his forty-day domination of Israel's army, Goliath had begun actually crossing the ravine and the base of the valley of Elah, and was coming up on Israel's side.

Goliath had been a bully and an intimidator his whole life. (Can you imagine him as a kid on the playground?) So he wasn't content to simply stand on the Philistine side jeering at Israel. He wasn't just down in the valley shouting up taunts. He was coming up on their turf, daring them to challenge him.

What do we learn from this? If you tolerate a giant, if you give him room, he will take over your territory. Before you know it he'll be right up on your doorstep—and then sleeping in your spare room. And in time he will seek to be the 'lord of the manor,' demanding your obedience.

If you give a little to the devil, he's going to want more. That's the way the game works. He will come to you and say, "Just give me this. It's a small thing. No big deal. You can have the rest. Just this. That's all. I don't want any more."

So you give in, and almost immediately he comes back and says, "Okay, so I lied. Now I want some more. Why are you surprised? What did you expect? Even Jesus called me the father of lies. Now yield me some more. Do it now!"

The truth is, he wants everything. He wants all of you. And if he can't take you to hell, he will at least try to bring hell to you. But he will start with a little so he can get a lot. That's why you don't want to give the devil a foothold in any way, shape, or form. That's why you don't want to run from giants, or tolerate their presence for days on end.

In Ephesians 4:27, Paul reminds us: "Do not give the devil a foothold" (NIV).

So what do you do with a giant?

You don't yell at it or threaten it or pretend to ignore it, you attack. You run at it and kill it as fast as you can. That's the only way to deal with it. You have to declare war on these things.

Look at 1 Samuel 17:48. "As Goliath moved closer to attack, David quickly ran out to meet him" (NLT).

I love that. As this colossus lumbered toward him, David was saying, "You want some of this, High-pockets? Let's go." He couldn't wait to get in Goliath's face. The Philistine giant may have expected the much smaller man to run around in circles and rely on his quickness and ability to dodge here and there. But that's not what happened. David ran right at him, and death was in his hand.

While David ran, he was whipping around that sling of his like a propeller, building up momentum. He'd had lots of practice at it. What else do you do when you're stuck in the wilderness with a bunch of dumb sheep for companions? You pray, play your tunes, and practice with your sling. After endless hours of perfecting his technique, he could probably knock a butterfly off a rock at fifty

paces. When lions or bears came out of the woods looking
for lamb chops, David could bring them down with
a single stone.

So what was Goliath? As far as David was concerned,
he was just another big, wild animal running amuck
amongst the sheep.

He let that stone rip like a guided missile and it sank
right into the giant's broad forehead. For the brief-
est of moments, Goliath was probably stunned. What
happened? What hit me? And then, like an old-growth
pine tree, he came crashing face first into the ground.

You see, David didn't waste time with feints and
dodges and fancy footwork. He didn't try to talk his
enemy to death. He ran right at that giant and let loose.

We need to do the same with the giants that confront
us. Let's say you face the giant of pornography. That's
a big one for many people these days—it's just so much
more accessible today than it has ever been before. There
you sit at your computer with no one around, and the
World Wide Web is before you. With just a few simple
clicks, you can call up images that no one should ever see.

And once you've been there, once you've given in, the
giant has access to beat you up again and again. I have
seen lives and marriages and whole families utterly
devastated and destroyed by Internet pornography.

Don't play with it. Don't toy with it. Don't coddle it. It
is powerful and it is dangerous and it is a creation of hell.

You need to attack it straight on. You need to bring it

out into the light of day. It starts when you put aside the pretenses and get honest with someone you trust. You talk about it. Nobody wants to do that, but you must do that. You have to attack this giant head-on or it will grind you to a pulp. You need to go to a Christian friend or your pastor and say, "I've got to level with you. I want to be up front. I can't hide it anymore. I have a problem with this thing, and I want you to hold me accountable. This is what I have done. And now I need help. Pray for me. Call me up and ask me how I'm doing. See if I'm messing around with it. Check my computer out if you want to, anytime at all. Ask me. Confront me. I am ready to flush this giant out and deal with it."

David fought Goliath in the light of day. And that's where we must fight our giants. Force it out into the light. Stop hiding it. Stop making excuses for it. Stop lying to yourself. Stop pretending it's not there. Recognize it. It is a giant, and it is going to destroy you and everyone you love if you don't take your stand. But remember where you're taking that stand: In the strength of the Lord and the power of His might. And then you are going to defeat that menacing enemy in the power and authority of the King of kings.

The devil doesn't want us to know these things. That's not hard to figure out. He wants to keep us trapped. He wants to keep us cowed and intimidated. He wants us to think that we're always going to be under the control of this vice or sin or problem.

In our distorted thinking, we somehow end up picturing God as a midget and Satan as some kind of great warrior. We need to get things back into their proper perspective and realize that Satan is nowhere near being the equal of God.

We need to remember and rely on the fact that Satan is a created being who was soundly defeated at the cross of Calvary. Prior to His crucifixion on the cross, Jesus said, "Now is the judgment of this world; now the ruler of this world will be cast out" (John 12:31). Referring to that same event on Calvary, Jesus said, "The ruler of this world is judged" (John 16:11). Through His death on the cross, Jesus destroyed him who held the power of death—the devil.

So what does all this mean?

Just this: It means you don't fight *for* victory. You fight *from* it.

You don't pray, "O Lord, please give me the victory, I pray." Instead, you pray, "Lord, thank You that the victory has been won at the cross of Calvary. I stand on that victory. I stand in the Lord and the power of His might. I've got my armor on now, heavenly Father. You won't give me more than I can handle. And I'm going to attack that giant, and by Your strength I'm going to see that giant come down."

That's what happened for a teenager named David, and thousands of years later, we still feel the effects of that act of faith.

Now if you and I had written the story of David and Goliath, it would probably go something like this. David gets called out of obscurity and is anointed king. (Small-town boy makes good.) He proves his courage and his skill in the valley of Elah, felling the great Philistine warrior in front of the whole army. He marries the king's daughter (throw in a little romance), and quickly ascends to the throne. And everyone lives happily ever after.

That's how we might write it. But that's not how the story goes at all.

David was by no means done with fighting giants.

But not all giants look the same, do they? Just when we think we've got the technique down for slaying nine-foot-six-inch brutes like Goliath, we meet up with a giant of a different kind altogether.

5 | *Don't Fight* ALONE

I don't know about you, but I'm just as happy not to know the future. The Lord has led me hour by hour, day by day, since I gave my heart to Him back in high school. And that's the way I like it.

Jesus tells us, "Therefore do not worry about tomorrow, for tomorrow will worry about itself. Each day has enough trouble of its own" (Matthew 6:34, NIV).

What a wealth of wisdom is wrapped up in those words. He is saying, "Deal with today, and that will be enough for you. I've given you all the grace you need to face this next twenty-four hours, with its problems, opportunities, and challenges. But if you try to wrestle with yesterday and tomorrow in addition to today, you'll be overwhelmed."

Remember this: the will of God will never take you where the grace of God will not protect you!

David had no idea of what was awaiting Him in the future after his great victory over Goliath. If he had known, he might have hired out as a shepherd somewhere far, far away. Like Egypt. Or Mars.

Maybe he felt lonely and unfulfilled out there on the backside of obscurity, watching over the family flock. But after he found himself caught up in the gears of national politics, after Saul had turned on him and began hunting him like an exhausted fox from one hole to another across the length and breadth of the land, he probably looked back on his shepherding stint as "the good old days." *Oh man, those were the days. All I had to deal with were bears and lions and sleeping out in the cold at night. But I had my harp, my poetry, my target practice, the stars at night, and the Lord was with me. What wonderful days those were.*

By all rights, killing the Philistine champion should have led to fame and fortune and popularity.

And it did.

For a while.

But when David began to demonstrate the Lord's favor on his life, Saul started seeing him as a threat. And that began a long, lean, mean string of fugitive years, staying on guard 24/7 just to save his skin. What killing Goliath had actually done for David was to lead him into one of the deepest, longest, darkest valleys of his life.

At this point, David was barely twenty. An overnight hero and celebrity, he became the hottest item in Israel. He was on the cover of *Time*, *Newsweek*, and *U.S. News and World Report*. *People Magazine* named him the sexiest giant-killer alive. He was on CBS, ABC, NBC, CNN, and Fox news. He was on with Bill O'Reilly and Larry King. He was on the speaking circuit, earning a quarter million a pop for his speeches.

At least, that's what would have happened if David lived in our era. He was the man. Everybody was talking about him. The number one song on Israeli radio was all about David and his exploits. To a nation hungry for victory and success, he had become a wildly popular personality.

That kind of instant adulation would have brought down a lot of people right then and there. But David took it all in stride. He handled it all so well.

But he had to face another giant. Not the lumbering Goliath; he was long gone. Now David had to put up with the paranoid, relentless attacks of jealous King Saul. For years and years to come, David would have no rest, no peace. Saul hunted him day and night. He promised to stop, and then went at it again the very next day.

Knowing David would need a friend to face this new giant, God provided a real blue chip guy: Prince Jonathan, the son of Saul. Jonathan was the very person to guide David through this strange, heady new environment of royalty, politics, and intrigue.

David might easily have been resistant to a friend from this quarter, imagining some sort of conspiracy or plot in the works, and not wanting anything to do with Saul or his kin. But the son of Jesse decided to make a friend out of an individual who should-have-been, could-have-been a natural enemy.

And Jonathan turned out to be the best friend he would ever have.

President Abraham Lincoln was criticized by an associate on one occasion regarding his attitude toward his enemies. "Why do you always make friends of them?" the associate asked the president. "You should destroy them."

Lincoln replied, "Am I not destroying my enemies when I make them my friends?"

Good response.

Life is hard enough without making unnecessary enemies. And if we can make an ally out of a onetime enemy, we are doubly blessed: gaining a friend and losing an adversary at the same time. The Scripture tells us in Romans,

> Never pay back evil for evil to anyone. Do things in such a way that everyone can see you are honorable. Do your part to live in peace with everyone, as much as possible.
>
> Dear friends, never avenge yourselves. Leave that to God. For it is written, "I will take vengeance; I will repay those who deserve it," says the Lord.
>
> Instead, do what the Scriptures say: "If your enemies are hungry, feed them. If they are thirsty, give them something to drink, and they will be ashamed of what they have done to you."
>
> Don't let evil get the best of you, but conquer evil by doing good. (12:17-21, NLT)

David tried to make a friend out of Saul, too, but the wicked king would have none of it. That's why I'm glad for the verse that says, "If it is possible, as much as depends on you, live peaceably with all men" (Romans 12:18).

Frankly, it's *not* always possible.

Some people just don't want a relationship with you, no matter what you say or do. Some people don't want to dialogue with you, hear your side of things, or even have a conversation with you. They want to be your enemy. Like it or not, there are people out there who thrive on hatred and meanness. Bitterly unhappy themselves, they're always looking for something new to complain about. You cannot appease a person like that. But as much as it lies in you, if it's at all possible, at least make an attempt to be a friend to a person like that, showing them the love of the Lord Jesus.

Jonathan and David had a special bond. They were best friends, and their hearts knit together. In fact, after Jonathan's tragic death in battle, David wrote: "I grieve for you, Jonathan my brother; you were very dear to me. Your love for me was wonderful, more wonderful than that of women" (2 Samuel 1:26, NIV).

Some cynical people with twisted minds have suggested there might have been more here than friendship, suggesting that David and Jonathan were actually homosexuals. This is so ridiculous it doesn't even deserve a response. No self-respecting Hebrew of this day living in a covenant with God would enter into a relationship like that. Considering the fact that David was a man after God's own heart, that would be the furthest thing from his thoughts. Clearly David was a man's man, and so attracted to women that it would eventually get him into a heap of trouble.

In this relationship between Jonathan and David, we learn a little bit about what friendship really ought to be. Here are a few things to consider.

A TRUE FRIEND IS *Willing to Sacrifice*

You don't have to beg a friend for a favor. You just ask. In fact, your friend might even be upset with you if you don't ask. If you had a crisis in your life, and you didn't go to your friend in your hour of need, he or she might be a little disappointed or irritated with you.

"Hey, we're friends! I've told you if you ever need anything to call me. Why did you try to ride this out alone?"

A friend wants to help, and doesn't shrink back from commitment. When Prince Jonathan wanted to show David the level of his allegiance, he took the royal robe off his shoulders and gave it to the former shepherd. He also gave him his armor—including his sword, his bow, and his belt. A true friend is there to assist you no matter what—without keeping score.

A TRUE FRIEND WILL *Staunchly Defend You*

Jonathan spoke well of David before his father Saul, who
had turned on him. In 1 Samuel 19 we read:

> The next morning Jonathan spoke with his father about
> David, saying many good things about him. "Please
> don't sin against David," Jonathan pleaded. "He's never
> done anything to harm you. He has always helped you
> in any way he could. Have you forgotten about the time
> he risked his life to kill the Philistine giant and how the
> LORD brought a great victory to Israel as a result? You
> were certainly happy about it then. Why should you
> murder an innocent man like David? There is no reason
> for it at all!" (vv. 4-5, NLT)

Jonathan had no illusions about what kind of man his
father was. He'd seen his dad's temper and instability. It
was a risk—even for Saul's own son and heir—to speak up
for David. But the young prince was ready to step into the
gap for his friend, in spite of the trouble it might cause.

Friends will not betray you. Friends will not be one
person to your face, and then another person as soon as
you leave the room. If the conversation suddenly turns
against you, a false friend will either clam up and say
nothing, or just go with the flow. That's a betrayal, and a
real friend won't do that. He or she will speak up for you,
even at the risk of getting hammered with anger or scorn.

As Oscar Wilde once said, "A true friend always stabs you in the front." An enemy stabs you in the back, but a friend stabs you in the front. In other words, a friend tells you the truth, to your face. Even when it hurts.

I am so thankful for friends who will listen to some of my wild ideas. I'll say, "Let me bounce something off you. Give me an honest read on this." And a true friend will do just that. You can trust them for a straight answer.

Let's say I bought a new shirt that I was thinking of wearing to some kind of event one night. And I ask you, "What do you think?"

You might reply, "Greg, I love you like a brother, but that's the worst-looking shirt I've ever seen on you. Take it back!" An enemy, on the other hand, would laugh up his sleeve and say, "Hey, you look great. Go for it. Wear it."

As the Scripture says in Proverbs 27:6, "Faithful are the wounds of a friend, but the kisses of an enemy are deceitful."

If you have a friend who loves you enough to confront you when you're doing the wrong thing or going the wrong direction, thank God for that person. Sure it's uncomfortable. For both of you! Most of us would rather say or hear things that are easy to receive. We don't like it when someone comes up to us and says, "I've been praying for you because I see an area in your life that could be a problem. I think you're going a little too far in this situation, or you're making some strategic mistakes over here, or I don't think that relationship is going to be helpful to you."

Now you could come back and say, "Mind your own business," or "Don't judge me." But as angry or embarrassed as you might be in that moment, you need to realize that this could be the best friend you've ever had. Your best friend may not be the person who agrees with everything you say and laughs at all of your jokes and always affirms you. It might be the person who out of love for you takes a risk and dares to tell you the truth.

David once wrote, "Let the righteous smite me in kindness and reprove me; it is oil upon the head; do not let my head refuse it" (Psalm 141:5, NASB). In other words, getting smacked alongside the head isn't always a bad thing, if it's from a real friend who's trying to wake you up and save you from heartache and disaster. "I won't refuse a punch like that," David says.

Do you have a friend who has been walking along the cliff edge of danger and self-destruction? If you see that danger and say nothing, not wanting to cause a scene or offend him or her, you're not a true friend at all. If you love someone, you'll risk anger, embarrassment, and even rejection to keep that person from destroying his or her life and family.

After you have committed the situation to the Lord in prayer, go to that person in humility and love, and say, "I could be off base here, and I could be reading this wrong, but here is what I see. Let me tell you my concern. . . ."

Prince Jonathan was loyal to David in the midst of intolerable circumstances. From the moment he pledged his friendship to David, he stayed in David's corner. It wasn't easy. It was uncomfortable, heartbreaking, and even dangerous. But he never wavered. So much so that many years after Jonathan's untimely death, David was still looking for ways to honor him and bless the remnants of his friend's family.

A true friend will be on your team even when you're not around to see it happen.

A TRUE FRIEND IS *an Encourager*

When David was down, when life was crumpling around him like a cardboard house in the rain, Jonathan did everything he could to stay in his life and lift him up.

The Bible says: "So David saw that Saul had come out to seek his life. And David was in the Wilderness of Ziph in a forest. Then Jonathan, Saul's son, arose and went to David in the woods and strengthened his hand in God. And he said to him, 'Do not fear, for the hand of Saul my father shall not find you. You shall be king over Israel, and I shall be next to you. Even my father Saul knows that.' So the two of them made a covenant before the LORD" (1 Samuel 23:15-18).

David was heartsick and afraid. No doubt his strong faith in God was being tested at that time as never before. He was in a dark and lonely place, and felt like all the world had gone against him. But Jonathan searched

David out to encourage him.

He went to David in the woods.

He searched for David in the wilderness.

It wasn't like he could punch in David's cell number, and give him a quick pep talk. He first had to go *find* his friend. The Bible doesn't tell us, but it's possible he had to search for a while, to check out a number of possible hiding places. Leaving his official duties like that might have put him in big trouble back home, but the thought of David out there in the woods, alone and fearful and discouraged, drove him on. Jonathan kept looking until he found him.

Are you that kind of friend? If you heard your friend was in some kind of trouble, would you be willing to keep looking for him even if had changed his address or didn't answer his phone? Would you keep after it even if your friend had found his way into some dark and uncomfortable places?

We like to think of the warm and sunny side of friendship, the times of laughter and conversation and mutual hobbies and shared dreams. But there is another side to genuine friendship, isn't there? And it isn't such a pleasant scene. It means hanging in there with someone who is off on a wrong path, or in trouble, or perhaps terminally ill.

A friend of mine told me about his experience when his wife had terminal cancer and was confined at home. Her two best friends, women who had been close to her for years, began to withdraw from her. They stopped calling, stopped coming around. It was too sad for them, too uncomfortable, too upsetting. So they simply stayed away. And my friend's wife had to face the deepest crisis of her life without the support of her two closest friends.

Don't turn away when your friend is facing a giant. Don't leave your friend to walk down into the Valley of Elah alone. Be there for him. Stand by her.

Pull your friend out of harm's way, even when it's uncomfortable or risky. The apostle Jude put it like this: "Be merciful to those who doubt; snatch others from the fire and save them; to others show mercy, mixed with fear—hating even the clothing stained by corrupted flesh" (v. 22-23, NIV).

What did Jonathan do when he finally found his fugitive friend in the wilderness? Scripture says he "strengthened David's hand in the Lord." He was saying, "Hang in there, David. You're God's man. You have destiny written all over you. Hold on to the Lord, trust in Him, and He will deliver you."

When I think of the word "encouragement," I think about someone who *breathes courage into the heart and life of another*.

Do you have a friend who encourages you? Someone you can call up when you're down? Someone who will seek you out when you find yourself in a dark and lonely place? Someone who will refresh your faith in the Lord when times look bleak?

Thank God for friends like that. Be a friend like that.

JUST *Do It*

Is there a giant in your life today? A giant who intimi-
dates you and taunts you? It might be formidable and
obvious like a Goliath. Or it might be more subtle and
sly like a Saul.

This world of ours is full of giants, full of opponents.
When you have openly committed yourself to Christ and
His purposes, values, and priorities on earth, enemies like
this come with the territory. But it's worth it. It is *always*
worth it.

If you find yourself in a season of extreme difficulty
right now, a period of disappointment and discourage-
ment, I would suggest to you that the Lord might be
preparing you today for something He will do in your life
tomorrow or beyond. You need to learn the lessons that
He has for you to learn in this valley you're in, this time of
difficulty. And if there is a particular area of your life that
is controlling you, oppressing you, tearing you down, or
blocking your path, it's time to face your giant.

It's time to realize the battle is not yours, but the Lord's.

It's time to call that giant out, force it out into the light
of day, attack it, and declare victory over it in the powerful
name of Jesus.

Maybe today is the day when that Goliath or Saul of
yours goes down for good.

Notes:

1. Alan Redpath, *The Making of a Man of God: Lessons from the Life of David* (Grand Rapids, Mich.: Fleming H. Revell Company, 2004)
2. Charles R. Swindoll, *David, Great Lives Series: Volume 1* (Nashville, Tenn.: W Publishing Group, 1997), p. 22

Other AllenDavid books
published by Kerygma Publishing

The Great Compromise

For Every Season: Daily Devotions

Strengthening Your Marriage

Marriage Connections

Are We Living in the Last Days?

"I'm Going on a Diet Tomorrow"

Strengthening Your Faith

Deepening Your Faith

Visit:

www.kerygmapublishing.com
www.allendavidbooks.com
www.harvest.org